Sequencing & Memory

Grades **PK-2**

CARSON-DELLOSA®
PUBLISHING GROUP

Greensboro, NC 27425 USA

Table of Contents

Brighter Child®
An imprint of Carson-Dellosa Publishing LLC
PO Box 35665
Greensboro, NC 27425 USA

ISBN 978-1-4838-1650-0

02-352177784

1 • one

Draw a line to match each number 1 to one thing.

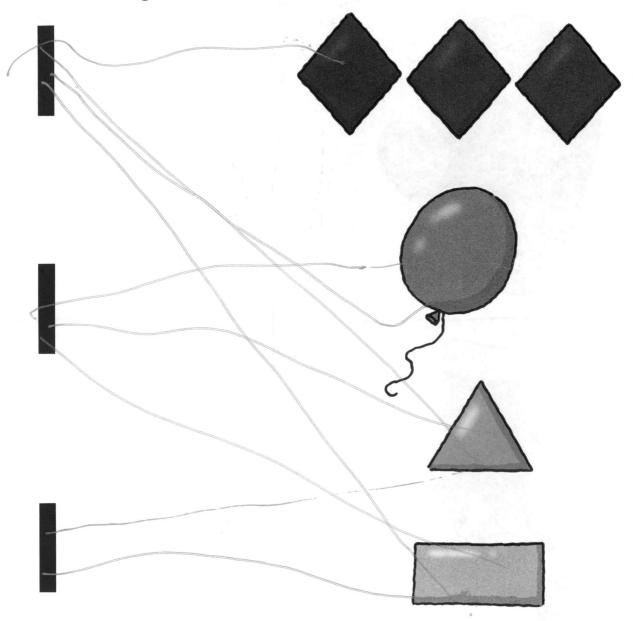

3

2 • • two

Draw another picture in each box to make **2** of each thing.

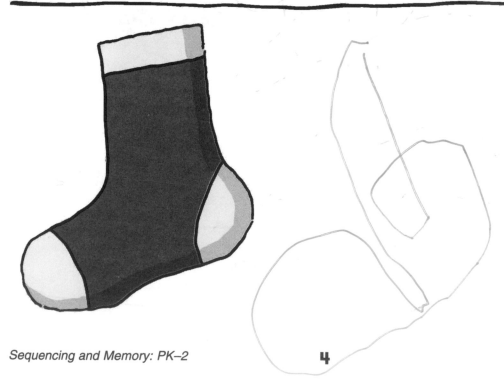

4

Name _____

3 • • • three

Circle **3** of each kind of cookie to go in the cookie jar.

4 • • • • four

Draw 4 flowers in the vase.

5 • • • • • five

Count the shapes. Draw more so that each box has **5** shapes in it. Write **5** on each line.

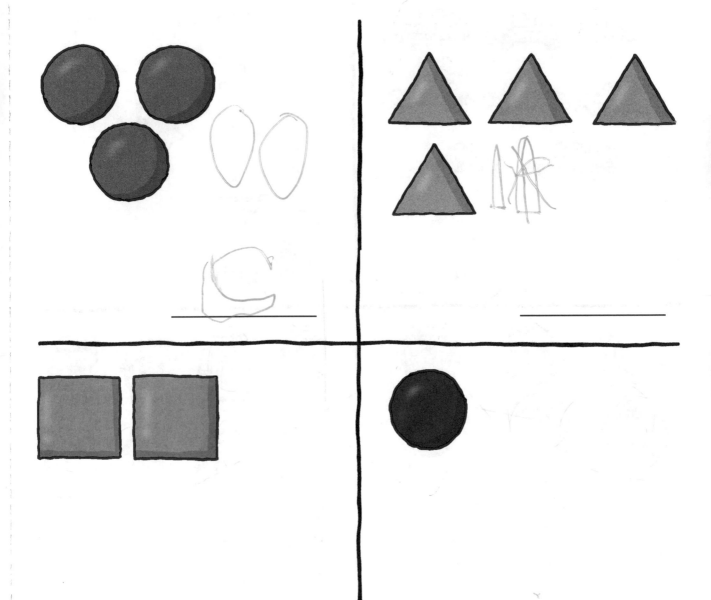

7

Sequencing and Memory: PK–2

6 ⦂⦂⦂ six

Circle **6** things in each box. Write the number **6** on each line.

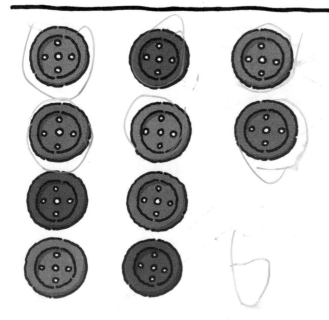

_____

_____

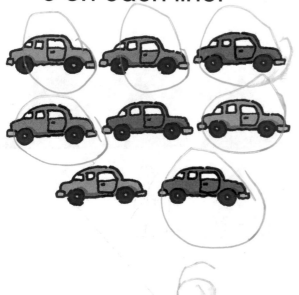

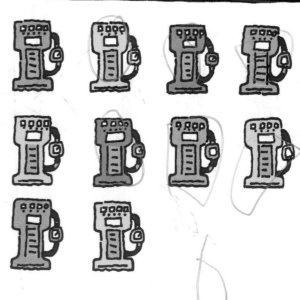

_____

_____

7 ⬤⬤⬤⬤⬤⬤⬤ seven

Circle **7** things on each shelf.

Sequencing and Memory: PK–2

8 ⠿ eight

Draw a line from each basket to the tree with the same number of apples.

q •••• ••••• nine

Circle 9 bugs in each group.

10 :::::: ten

Draw 10 legs on the caterpillar.

Look at the big picture below. Then, look at the small pictures. Circle the small picture that shows what will happen **next**.

Name _____

FIRST, NEXT, LAST

Number the pictures below to show what happened **first**, **next** and **last**.

- Write 1 under the picture that happened **first**.
- Write 2 under the picture that happened **next**.
- Write 3 under the picture that happened **last**.

1 2 3

FIRST, NEXT, LAST

Number the pictures below to show what happened **first**, **next** and **last**.

- Write 1 under the picture that happened **first**.
- Write 2 under the picture that happened **next**.
- Write 3 under the picture that happened **last**.

8 8

2   2 3   1

ORDINAL NUMBERS

Circle the **third** person in line. Draw a line under the **second** person.

Draw an **X** on the **first** person on the bench. Draw a hat on the **fifth** person.

16

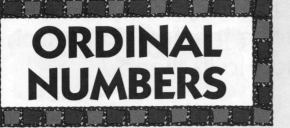

ORDINAL NUMBERS

Draw an **X** on the **fifth** tree. Draw a box around the **third** tree.

Draw a line under the **second** tree. Circle the **first** tree.

Name _____

Each dog needs a bone.
Trace the line from each
dog to its bone.

ONE-TO-ONE CORRESPONDENCE

Trace the string from the cat to the ball of yarn. Then draw more balls of yarn so each cat has one to play with.

MORE AND FEWER

Count the blocks each child is playing with. Circle the child who has **more** blocks.

Name _____

Count the blocks in each group. Circle the group of blocks that has **more**.

Sequencing and Memory: PK–2

MORE AND FEWER

Count the blocks in the first box. Then draw a group of blocks that has **more**.

Comparing: Few and Many

Directions: Color the parts of the clown that contain many more than the other side. Be sure to check the clown's hat, collar, suit, and shoes.

Name _____

PATTERNS

Complete the shape patterns. At the end of the row, draw the shape that comes next. Then, color the shape.

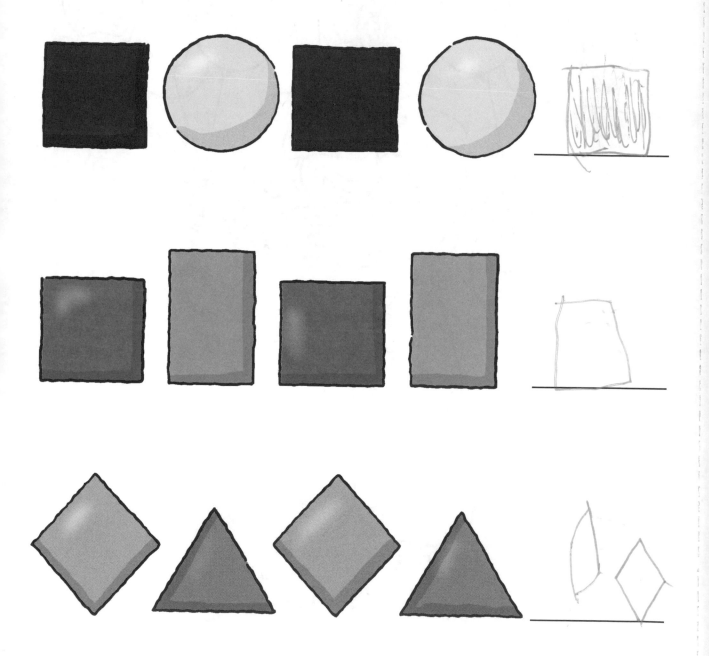

PATTERNS

Complete the picture patterns. At the end of the row, draw the picture that comes next.

PATTERNS

Complete the letter patterns. At the end of the row, write the letter that comes next.

L L H L L _H_

V V X V V _X_

B B D B B _D_

Name _____

Complete the picture patterns. Draw what is missing on the last picture in each row.

Patterns

Directions: Look at the shapes. Draw and color the shape that comes next in each pattern.

Patterns

Directions: Look at the patterns. Draw the shape that comes next.

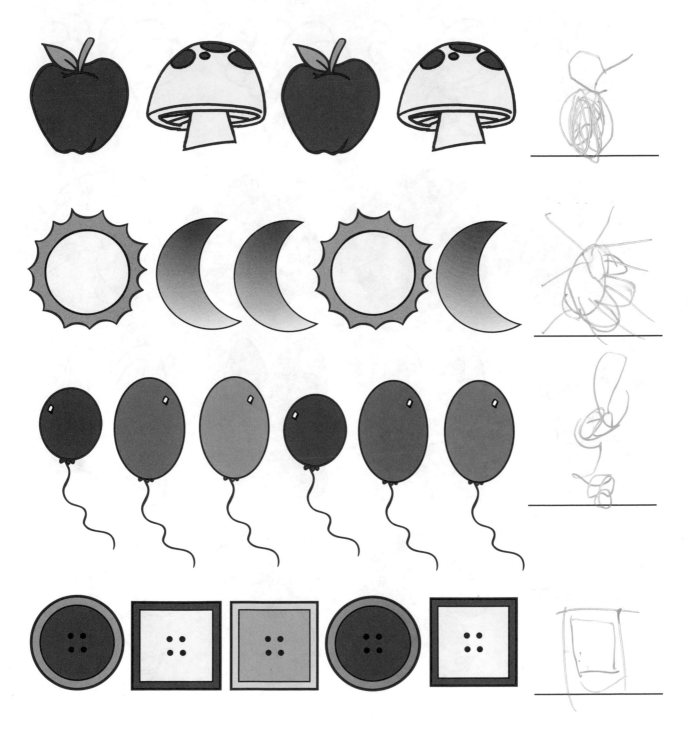

Patterns

Directions: Complete the pattern by coloring the last shape.

Patterns

Directions: Look at the patterns. Write the letter that comes next.

A a A a A a __

T z z T __

H H H c H __

f f e e __

Name _____

Look at the pictures in each row. Circle the picture that goes together with the first picture.

Name _____

Look at the pictures in each row. Circle the picture that goes together with the first picture.

Name _____

Look at the pictures in each row. Circle the picture that is the **same** as the first picture in each row.

Name _____

DIFFERENT

Look at the pictures in each row. Circle the picture that is **different** in each row.

SAME

Look at the shapes in each row. Color the shape that is the **same** as the first shape in each row.

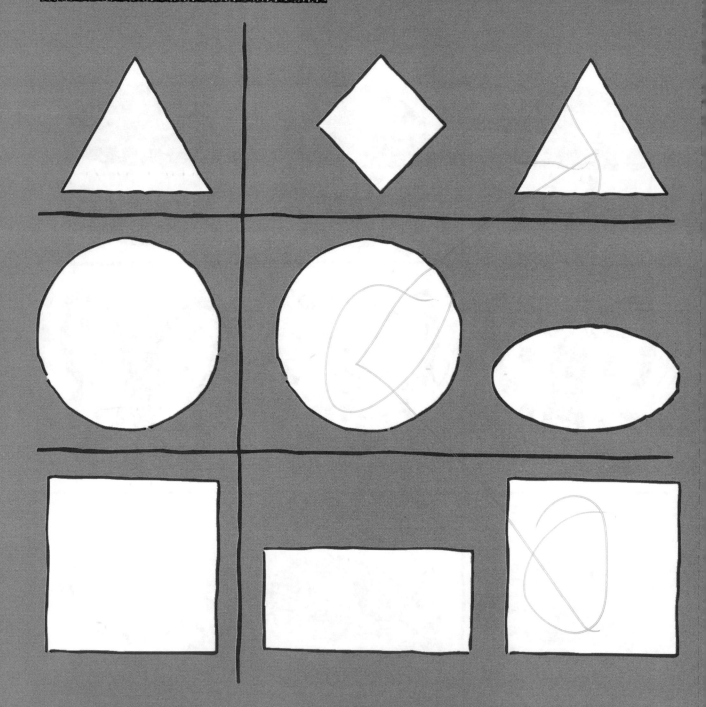

Color the shape in each
row that is **different**.

DIFFERENT

Name _____

SAME

Look at the letters in each row. Circle the letter that is the **same** as the first letter in each row.

E   F   E

R   B   R

M   M   N

Same and Different

Directions: Color the shape that looks the same as the first shape in each row.

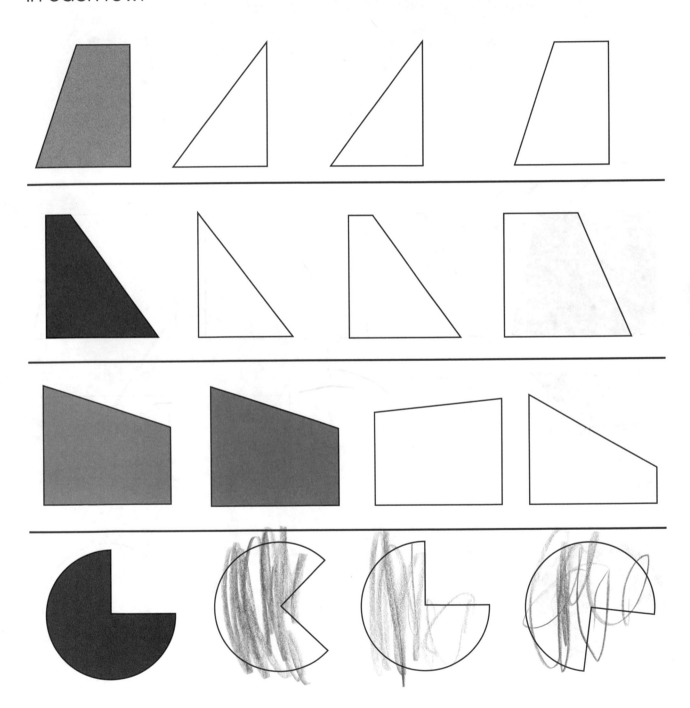

Same and Different

Directions: Draw an **X** on the shapes in each row that do not match the first shape.

40

Same and Different

Directions: Color the shape in each row that does not belong.

Example:

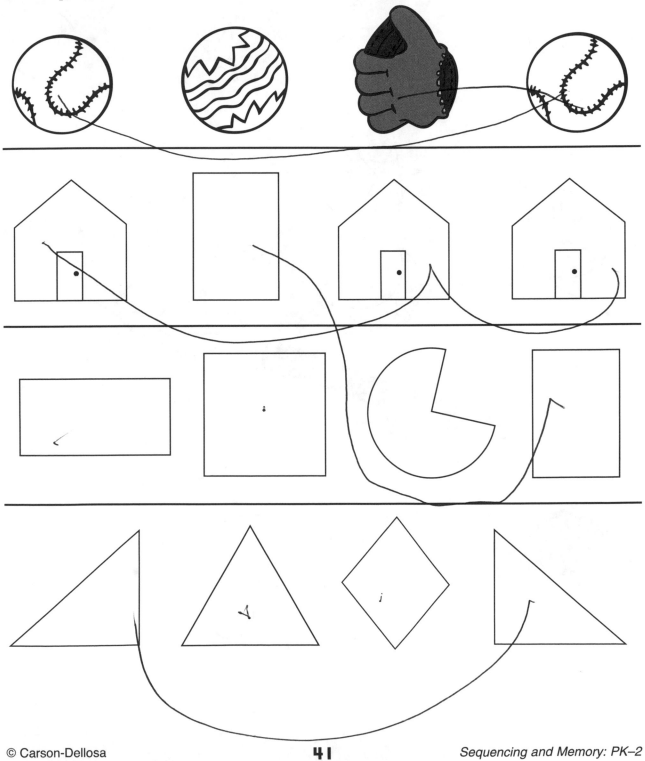

Classifying

Bob is looking for stars. Help him find them.
Directions: Color all the stars blue.

How many stars did you and Bob find? _____

Classifying

Directions: Color the stars. How many stars?_____

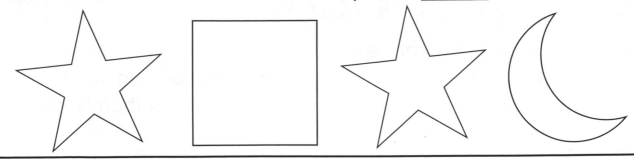

Color the moons. How many moons?_____

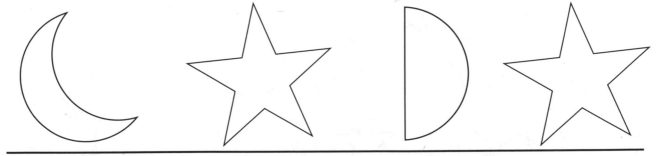

Directions: Color the half-circles. How many half-circles?_____

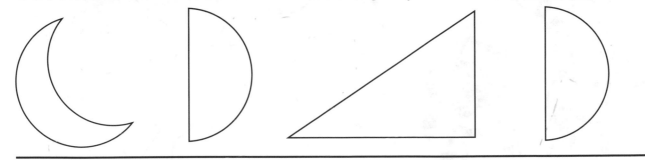

Color the rhombuses. How many rhombuses?_____

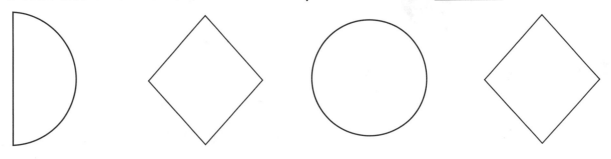

Classifying

Marnie and Kyle are taking a trip into space. Help them find the stars, moons, circles, and rhombuses.

Directions: Color the shapes.

Use yellow for stars.   Use blue for moons.

Use red for circles.   Use purple for rhombuses.

Directions: Write the numbers.

How many stars? _____   How many moons? _____

How many circles? _____   How many rhombuses? _____

Classifying

Help Martha and Doug sort their shapes.

Directions: Draw a line from each shape to the basket where it belongs.

45

Classifying

Directions: Look at the shapes. Answer the questions.

How many white shapes?   _____

How many blue shapes?   _____

How many half-white shapes?   _____

How many blue stars?   _____

How many white circles?   _____

Classifying

Directions: Find some pencils, pens, straws, toothpicks, paper clips and crayons. Count them. Write the number.

How many:

pencils ? _____   straws ? _____

paper clips ? _____   pens ✒ ? _____

toothpicks ╱ ? _____   crayons ▬ ? _____

Draw a picture of each thing you found.

_____
| |
| |
| |
| |
| |
| |
| |
|_____|

Classifying

Directions: Look at the shapes with Misty. Then, answer the questions.

How many stars? _____

How many circles? _____

How many half-circles? _____

How many moons? _____

How many squares? _____

How many triangles? _____

How many rhombuses? _____

Observation

Directions: Draw a line from each animal to its shadow.

Observation

Directions: Color the object that matches the shadow at the beginning of each row.

Observation

Directions: Find these hidden objects in the picture. Circle them. Then, color the picture.

Observation

Directions: Ten things in picture 1 are missing from picture 2. Draw them in picture 2. Then, color the picture.

Thinking Skills

Directions: Draw an **X** on the object in each row that does not belong. Color the ones that belong together.

Thinking Skills

Directions: Circle the eight objects that do not belong in the picture. Draw three things that could go in the picture.

54

Thinking Skills

Directions: Draw the missing part of each object.

Thinking Skills

Directions: Follow the dots in abc order. Draw a line from each small picture to the dot-to-dot where it belongs.

Name _____

CRITICAL THINKING

Let your child color and cut apart the cards below. Then have him or her put the cards in the correct order. Fasten them together to make a book.

CRITICAL THINKING

Let your child color and cut apart the cards below. Then have him or her put the cards in a straight line according to size.

CRITICAL THINKING

Let your child color and cut apart the cards below. Then have him or her put the cards in the correct order. Fasten them together to make a book.

62

Name _____

Let your child color and cut apart the cards below. Then have him or her put the cards in the correct order. Fasten them together to make a book.

Name _____

CRITICAL THINKING

Let your child draw and color details on the trees below according to each season of the year. Then have him or her cut the cards apart and put them in correct order. Fasten them together to make a book.

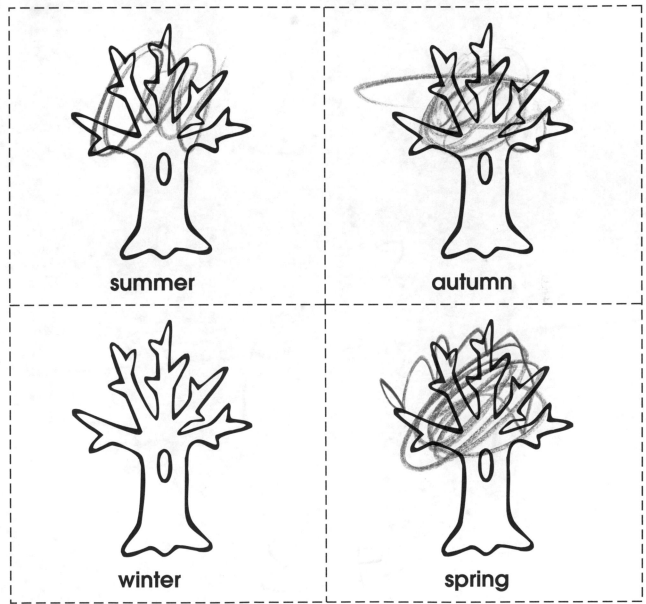

summer

autumn

winter

spring

Sequencing and Memory: PK–2

66

Name _____

Color and cut apart the cards below. Ask your child to match each mother to its baby.

horse   duck   pig

hen   cow   sheep

piglet   chick   foal

duckling   lamb   calf

68

Name ______________________________

Following Directions: Shapes and Colors

Directions: Color the picture.

Use red for the □'s.

Use blue for the ○'s.

Use purple for the △'s.

Use green for the D's.

Use yellow for the ☆'s.

Use black for the ♡'s.

Use pink for the ◇'s.

1 · one

Draw a line to match each number 1 to one thing.

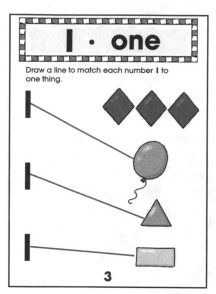

3

2 ·· two

Draw another picture in each box to make 2 of each thing.

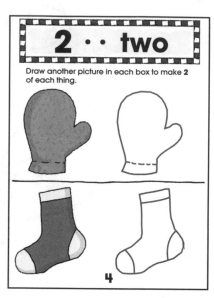

4

3 ··· three

Circle 3 of each kind of cookie to go in the cookie jar.

5

4 ···· four

Draw 4 flowers in the vase.

6

5 ····· five

Count the shapes in each box. Draw more so that each box has 5 shapes in it. Write 5 on each line.

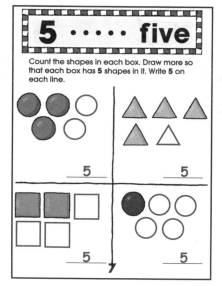

7

6 ⠿ six

Circle 6 things in each box. Write the number 6 on each line.

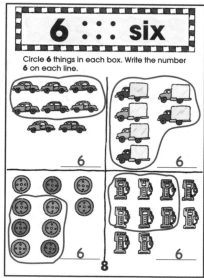

8

7 :::: **seven**

Circle **7** things on each shelf.

9

8 :::: **eight**

Draw a line from each basket to the tree with the same number of apples.

10

9 :::: **nine**

Circle **9** bugs in each group.

11

10 :::: **ten**

Draw **10** legs on the caterpillar.

12

NEXT

Look at the big picture below. Then look at the small pictures. Circle the small picture that shows what will happen **next**.

13

FIRST NEXT, LAST

Number the pictures below to show what happened **first**, **next** and **last**.
- Write 1 under the picture that happened **first**.
- Write 2 under the picture that happened **next**.
- Write 3 under the picture that happened **last**.

3   1   2

14

Sequencing and Memory: PK–2

FIRST NEXT, LAST

Number the pictures below to show what happened **first**, **next** and **last**.
- Write 1 under the picture that happened **first**.
- Write 2 under the picture that happened **next**.
- Write 3 under the picture that happened **last**.

2   3   1

15

ORDINAL NUMBERS

Circle the **third** person in line. Draw a line under the **second** person.

Draw an **X** on the **first** person on the bench. Draw a hat on the **fifth** person.

16

ORDINAL NUMBERS

Draw an **X** on the **fifth** tree. Draw a box around the **third** tree.

Draw a line under the **second** tree. Circle the **first** tree.

17

ONE-TO-ONE CORRESPONDENCE

Each dog needs a bone. Trace the line from each dog to its bone.

18

ONE-TO-ONE CORRESPONDENCE

Trace the string from the cat to the ball of yarn. Then draw more balls of yarn so each cat has one to play with.

19

MORE AND FEWER

Count the blocks each child is playing with. Circle the child who has **more** blocks.

20

MORE AND FEWER

Count the blocks in each group. Circle the group of blocks that has **more**.

21

MORE AND FEWER

Count the blocks in the first box. Then draw a group of blocks that has **more**.

A B C

22

Comparing: Few and Many

Directions: Color the parts of the clown that contain many more than the other side. Be sure to check the clown's hat, collar, suit and shoes.

23

PATTERNS

Complete the shape patterns. At the end of the row, draw the shape that comes next. Then color the shape.

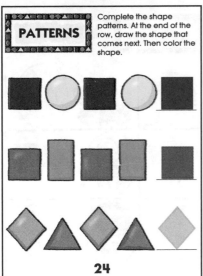

24

PATTERNS

Complete the picture patterns. At the end of the row, draw the picture that comes next.

25

PATTERNS

Complete the letter patterns. At the end of the row, write the letter that comes next.

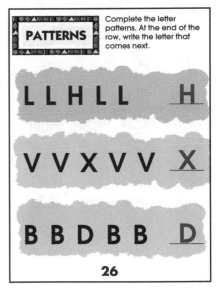

L L H L L H

V V X V V X

B B D B B D

26

PATTERNS

Complete the picture patterns. Draw what is missing on the last picture in each row.

27

Patterns

Directions: Look at the shapes. Draw and color the shape that comes next in each pattern.

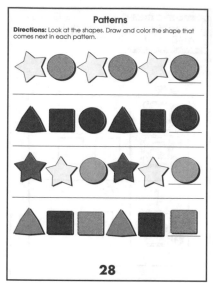

28

Patterns

Directions: Look at the patterns. Draw the shape that comes next.

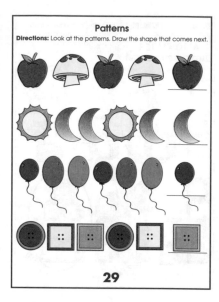

29

Patterns

Directions: Complete the pattern by coloring the last shape.

30

Patterns

Directions: Look at the patterns. Write the letter that comes next.

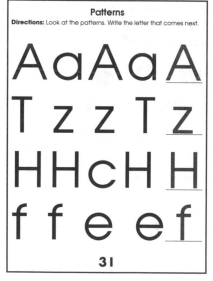

A a A a A __

T z z T z __

H H c H H __

f f e e f __

31

GO-TOGETHERS

Look at the pictures in each row. Circle the picture that goes together with the first picture.

32

GO-TOGETHERS

Look at the pictures in each row. Circle the picture that goes together with the first picture.

33

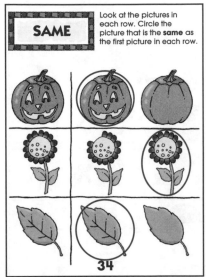

SAME

Look at the pictures in each row. Circle the picture that is the **same** as the first picture in each row.

34

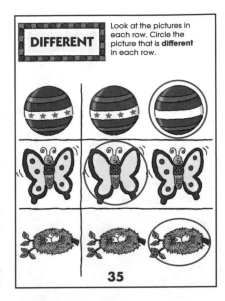

DIFFERENT

Look at the pictures in each row. Circle the picture that is **different** in each row.

35

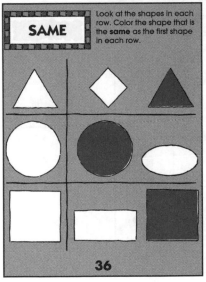

SAME

Look at the shapes in each row. Color the shape that is the **same** as the first shape in each row.

36

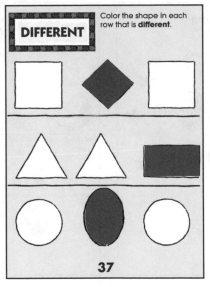

DIFFERENT

Color the shape in each row that is **different**.

37

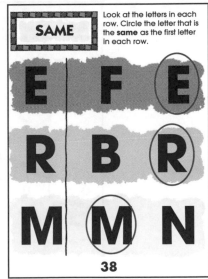

SAME

Look at the letters in each row. Circle the letter that is the **same** as the first letter in each row.

38

Same and Different

Directions: Color the shape that looks the same as the first shape in each row.

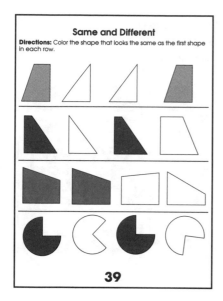

39

Same and Different

Directions: Draw an **X** on the shapes in each row that do not match the first shape.

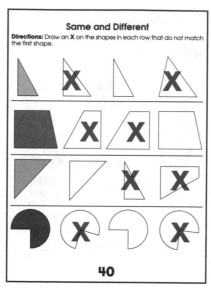

40

Same and Different

Directions: Color the shape in each row that does not belong.

Example:

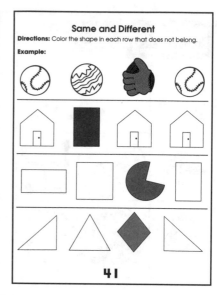

41

Classifying

Bob is looking for stars. Help him find them.
Directions: Color all the stars blue.

How many stars did you and Bob find? __10__

42

Classifying

Directions: Color the stars. How many stars? __2__

Color the moons. How many moons? __1__

Directions: Color the half-circles. How many half-circles? __2__

Color the rhombuses. How many rhombuses? __2__

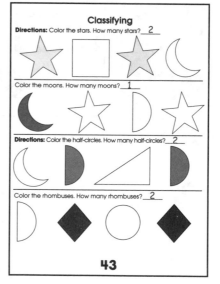

43

Classifying

Marnie and Kyle are taking a trip into space. Help them find the stars, moons, circles and rhombuses.

Directions: Color the shapes.

Use yellow for stars.
Use red for circles.

Use blue for moons.
Use purple for rhombuses.

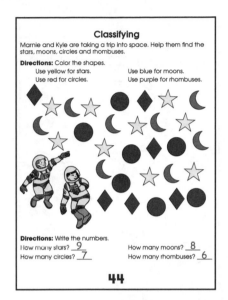

Directions: Write the numbers.

How many stars? __9__
How many circles? __7__

How many moons? __8__
How many rhombuses? __6__

44

Classifying

Help Martha and Doug sort their shapes.

Directions: Draw a line from each shape to the basket where it belongs.

45

Classifying

Directions: Look at the shapes. Answer the questions.

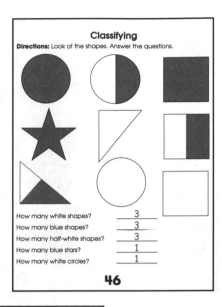

How many white shapes? __3__
How many blue shapes? __3__
How many half-white shapes? __3__
How many blue stars? __1__
How many white circles? __1__

46

Classifying

Directions: Find some pencils, pens, straws, toothpicks, paper clips and crayons. Count them.

How many:
pencils ✏ ?

Answers will vary.

paper clips
tooth

crayons ?

Draw a picture of each thing you found.

Drawings will vary.

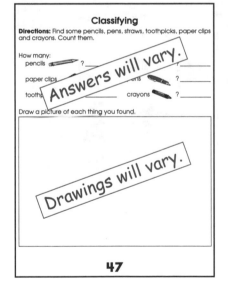

47

Classifying

Directions: Look at the shapes with Misty. Then answer the questions.

How many stars? __5__
How many circles? __3__
How many half-circles? __4__
How many moons? __6__
How many squares? __7__
How many triangles? __4__
How many rhombuses? __6__

48

---

77 *Sequencing and Memory: PK–2*

Observation

Directions: Draw a line from each animal to its shadow.

49

Observation

Directions: Color the object that matches the shadow at the beginning of each row.

50

Observation

Directions: Find these hidden objects in the picture. Circle them. Then color the picture.

Coloring will vary.

51

Observation

Directions: Ten things in picture 1 are missing from picture 2. Draw them in picture 2. Then color the picture.

52

Thinking Skills

Directions: Draw an **X** on the object in each row that does not belong. Color the ones that belong together.

53

Thinking Skills

Directions: Circle the eight objects that don't belong in the picture. Draw three things that could go in the picture.

54

Thinking Skills

Directions: Draw the missing part of each object.

55

Thinking Skills

Directions: Follow the dots in abc order. Draw a line from each small picture to the dot-to-dot where it belongs.

56

CRITICAL THINKING

Let your child color and cut apart the cards below. Then have him or her put the cards in the correct order. Fasten them together to make a book.

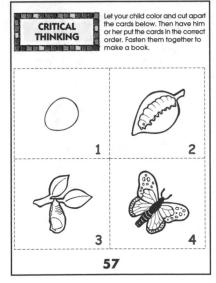

1   2

3   4

57

CRITICAL THINKING

Let your child color and cut apart the cards below. Then have him or her put the cards in a straight line according to size.

1   2   3

4   5   6

59

CRITICAL THINKING

Let your child color and cut apart the cards below. Then have him or her put the cards in the correct order. Fasten them together to make a book.

Goldilocks Three Bears

1 2
3 4

61

CRITICAL THINKING

Let your child color and cut apart the cards below. Then have him or her put the cards in the correct order. Fasten them together to make a book.

1 2
3 4

63

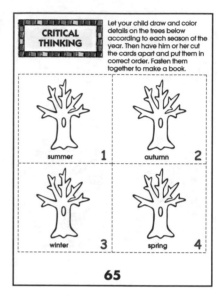

CRITICAL THINKING

Let your child draw and color details on the trees below according to each season of the year. Then have him or her cut the cards apart and put them in correct order. Fasten them together to make a book.

summer 1 autumn 2
winter 3 spring 4

65

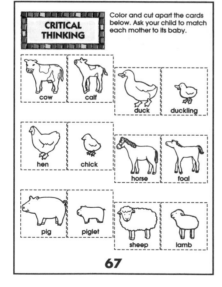

CRITICAL THINKING

Color and cut apart the cards below. Ask your child to match each mother to its baby.

cow calf duck duckling
hen chick horse foal
pig piglet sheep lamb

67

Following Directions: Shapes and Colors

Directions: Color the picture.

Use red for the □'s.
Use blue for the ○'s.
Use purple for the △'s.
Use green for the ◗'s.
Use yellow for the ☆'s.
Use black for the ♡'s.
Use pink for the ◇'s.

69